Shoes and Boots

through History

by
Fiona MacDonald

GARETH STEVENS
GS
PUBLISHING
A Member of the WRC Media Family of Companies

Please visit our web site at: www.garethstevens.com
For a free color catalog describing Gareth Stevens Publishing's
list of high-quality books and multimedia programs, call
1-800-542-2595 (USA) or 1-800-387-3178 (Canada).
Gareth Stevens Publishing's fax: (414) 332-3567.

Library of Congress Cataloging-in-Publication Data available upon request from publisher.
Fax (414) 336-0157 for the attention of the Publishing Records Department.

ISBN-10: 0-8368-6857-9 — ISBN-13: 978-0-8368-6857-9 (lib. bdg.)

This North American edition first published in 2007 by
Gareth Stevens Publishing
A Member of the WRC Media Family of Companies
330 West Olive Street, Suite 100
Milwaukee, Wisconsin 53212 USA

This edition copyright © 2007 by Gareth Stevens, Inc. Original edition copyright © 2006
by ticktock Entertainment Ltd. First published in Great Britain by ticktock Media Ltd.,
Unit 2 Orchard Business Centre, North Farm Road, Tunbridge Wells, Kent TN2 3XF.

Managing editor: Valerie J. Weber
Gareth Stevens editor: Gini Holland
Gareth Stevens art direction: Tammy West
Gareth Stevens designer: Kami Strunsee

Picture Credits (t=top, b=bottom, l=left, r=right, c=center):
Bridgeman Art Archive: title page, 20-21 all, 23 all; CORBIS: title page, 14 all, 15t, 24-25 all; Fort Rock Museum:
6b; Shutterstock: cover, 4b, 5 all; ticktock Media Image Archive: 4t, 7b, 12r, 13 all, 22 all, 26-27 all, 28-29 all;
Werner Forman Archive: 6t, 7t, 8-9 all, 10t, 10-11c, 11 t, 11b, 15br, 15bl, 16-17 all, 18-19 all; Yorvik Museum: 12l

Every effort has been made to trace the copyright holders, and we apologize in advance for any unintentional omission.
We would be pleased to insert the appropriate acknowledgements in any subsequent edition of this publication.

Printed in the United States of America

1 2 3 4 5 6 7 8 9 10 09 08 07 06

Table of Contents

Cover: An in-line skater wears special plastic boots with built-in wheels.

Words that appear in the glossary are printed in **boldface** type the first time they occur in the text.

Introduction

Humans are the only animals to design and make footwear. Why do people choose to wear coverings on their feet? Shoes and boots have practical purposes. They keep feet warm, dry, and protected. They also change the way people look. Shoes can make people look rich or poor, sporty or formal, business-like or glamorous.

Barefoot History

Shoes, boots, socks, and sandals are all fairly recent inventions for humans. For millions of years, men, women, and children walked barefoot as animals do. When people migrated to colder climates, they needed to make footwear to keep their feet warm.

The early ancestors of modern humans left footprints behind at Olduvai Gorge in Tanzania, Africa. The figures shown here are based on information gained from fossil footprints.

Sports Footwear

For two thousand years or more, special footwear has been designed for sports and exciting outdoor pastimes. Sports footwear gives support to players' feet and ankles. Some sports footwear can also help people move faster.

In-line skates have rigid plastic boots and fast-turning wheels.

Extreme Footwear

In the late twentieth century, new kinds of footwear were designed to work in extreme environments, such as in forest fires and undersea explorations. In the low gravity of the Moon, heavy boots helped keep astronauts grounded.

Moon boots, worn on the first lunar landing in 1969, had heavy soles to help astronauts walk normally in the Moon's low gravity.

Flattering Footwear

Heels on boots and shoes increase the wearer's height and make legs look longer. They also throw the body slightly out of balance, creating a swaying, forward-tilting walk. Many women think this kind of walk makes them look attractive, delicate, and feminine. Others just worry about falling!

A teenage girl considers wearing a high-heel shoe.

The First Shoes

When did people first begin to use footwear? The first shoes or boots were probably made between 50,000 B.C. and 20,000 B.C. The oldest known image of people wearing foot coverings comes from a rock painting in Spain made about 15,000 years ago.

Skins and Fibers

The first footwear was made of the same materials as other early clothing — animal skins and plant fibers. People wrapped strips of **hide** or fur around their feet and lower legs and held them in place with rawhide laces. In cold climates, this covering kept feet and legs warm. Plant fibers, such as **bark** and dried grass, were twisted together to make simple sandals. Sandals protected feet from thorns, stones, biting insects, and, in hot climates, burning sand.

Traditional sandals — made from plant fibers by Aboriginal people in Australia —still follow very ancient designs.

Woven Soles

By about 10,000 B.C., footwear designs had become more sophisticated. **Soles** for sandals were woven to fit the precise shape of the foot. These soles were fastened over the **instep** and around the ankle by neat strings of twisted plant fiber.

The oldest surviving footwear so far discovered is a pair of sandals found at Fort Rock, Oregon, dating from between 10,500 B.C. and 9300 B.C.

These bearskin and deerskin boots with grass and net padding were found on the frozen body of "Utzi," a man who died in the mountains of Italy in about 3300 B.C.

Laces and Insulation

The first **laced** shoes were made at least 7,000 years ago. They were made from a piece of animal hide pierced with holes around the edge. A thin **lace,** or narrow strip, of rawhide was threaded through holes and then pulled tightly to gather the shoe around the foot. By about 3500 B.C., boots were made with separate soles and **uppers**.

How did the Fort Rock shoes survive so long?

Knee-High Boots

The first boots covered only the feet and ankles. Each boot was worn with a **legging** that had a special flap attached. This flap extended to cover the top part of the foot and could be tucked inside the boot lacing. By about 1000 B.C., high boots were made by joining leggings, soles, and uppers together. These covered the feet and all of the lower legs as far as the knees.

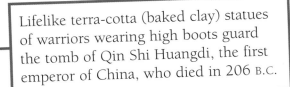

Lifelike terra-cotta (baked clay) statues of warriors wearing high boots guard the tomb of Qin Shi Huangdi, the first emperor of China, who died in 206 B.C.

Ancient Egypt and Its Neighbors

I n many early societies, such as in ancient Egypt, footwear was a sign of status. Only rich people could afford to purchase shoes or sandals, and only royal or noble families were allowed to wear them all the time.

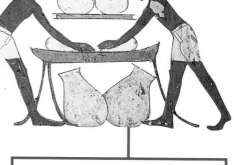

These Egyptian men are not wearing any shoes while baking bread. This was usual practice in ancient Egypt.

Going Barefoot

Most ordinary Egyptian men and all Egyptian women went barefoot both inside and outside. In the hot, dry climate of Egypt, their feet did not get wet or cold, but they did get cut, bruised, dusty, and dirty. Egyptian medical texts contain many remedies for sore, aching feet.

A Pharaoh's Footwear

The ancient Egyptians buried their pharaohs, or kings, and nobles in magnificent tombs with everything they would need in the **afterlife**, including shoes. Sandals were the most common footwear design. Most had a flat sole, **toe post**, and wide straps over the instep or around the heel. A pharaoh's sandals might be made of gold.

This gold statue of Pharaoh Tutankhamen shows him wearing typical ancient Egyptian sandals. Pharaohs' sandals were often decorated with gold and precious stones.

An Expert Trade

Egyptian sandals were made by expert **artisans**. They used a wide variety of materials, including wood, **palm fronds**, burlap cloth, and braided **papyrus**, which is a kind of river reed. Egyptians were some of the first people to use **tanned leather**. Some examples of their leather shoes are more than 5,000 years old!

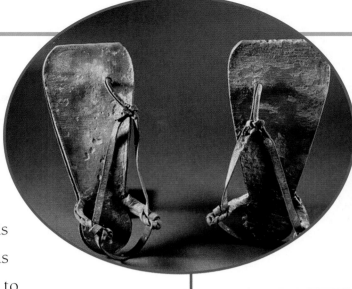

These Egyptian tanned-leather sandals were made in about 3000 B.C.

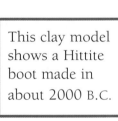

This clay model shows a Hittite boot made in about 2000 B.C.

Climbing and Riding

Many neighboring western Asian peoples had to survive in high mountains and cold weather. They developed footwear that was suitable for climbing up steep, snowy paths or for riding long distances. For example, Hittite mountain villagers — who lived in Turkey in about 2000 B.C. — made tough ankle boots with turned-up toes.

Who wore high heels in ancient Egypt?

Ancient Greece and Rome

A ncient Greece bordered the Mediterranean Sea, so ships from many European and western Asian civilizations called at Greek ports. Greek travelers and traders learned leather-working and shoe-making technologies from neighboring peoples.

This marble female foot dressed in a sandal dates from about the first or the second century A.D.

Female Fashions

Greek footwear was made from soft leather smoothed and polished with pork fat or olive oil. It was often brightly colored with plant dyes. For women, fashionable styles included slippers; open-toed shoes; **mules**, which were shoes without heel backs; shoes with thick cork soles; and sandals.

Styles for Men

Greek men also wore sandals. For long journeys, however, they put on walking shoes with thick, **hobnailed** soles or short, lace-up boots that protected their feet and gave extra support to their ankles.

Rough Country

This modern reproduction of a Roman *caliga* shows its thick sole.

In wartime, Greek warriors protected their legs with curved **greaves**, or shin plates. Greaves were made of metal for rich men or of thick, boiled leather for ordinary soldiers. They fastened behind the legs with leather straps and buckles and were worn with short, lace-up boots or heavy sandals.

The ancient Romans lived in Italy. At the peak of Roman power — about A.D. 100 — their capital city, Rome, housed over a million people. City inhabitants included expert shoemakers. They invented the first shoes designed to fit right or left feet only.

Soldiers' Sandals

Roman sandals could be lightweight — just a thin sole with slender straps — or heavy versions of calf-high army boots with the toes left open. Egyptian-style sandals, made of braided palm fronds, were mostly worn by actors. They were also worn by priests and philosophers as a sign of humility.

This Roman soldier wears calf-high army boots with the toes left exposed.

Caligae and Calcaei

For outdoor wear, the most important foot coverings were *caligae*, which were shoes or boots with thick, hobnailed soles made of many layers of leather, and *calcaei*, which were flat leather shoes shaped like ballet slippers. Calcaei could only be worn by high-ranking Romans.

Where did our word sandal *originate?*

Slippers and Socks

Romans were also some of the first people in the world to wear socks, called **udones**. These were boot shapes cut out of tightly-woven fabric and then carefully stitched together. Indoors, Romans wore udones alone, but outdoors, they wore them inside boots or sandals.

A bronze statue shows a lower leg clothed in a woven woolen sock and a simple sandal.

Medieval Europe

Ancient shoemaking traditions survived for centuries in Europe during the Middle Ages, or medieval times. In the far north, Vikings still wore fur-lined boots. In the far south, some people wore Roman-style sandals. In addition to these old styles, new footwear fashions developed.

Viking Footwear

Throughout Europe, most men and women wore new-style shoes that covered the whole foot to just below the ankle. These were convenient to wear with pants or with long, full skirts. They slipped on and off easily and fastened by means of a flap at one side. The flap was secured by leather ties or a wooden toggle.

Found in the Viking city of York in England, this leather shoe with its flap fastening dates from about A.D. 850.

Heavy Metal

During the early medieval period, soldiers wore their own everyday footwear in battle. In later years, wealthy knights from noble families paid for tailor-made suits of armor to protect them from head to toe. Covered in metal, their feet were safe from injury, but they were very heavy!

This medieval suit of armor features shoes called *sabatons*.

Leg Protection

Ordinary men and women who worked the land needed protection from cold, dampness, and thorny plants. They could not afford socks or high leather boots that reached to the knee. They wore simple, flat shoes and protected their lower legs with bands of cloth or sheepskin.

How long were the points on medieval men's shoes?

High Fashion

Wealthy men and women wore many different styles of fine leather shoes with shapes that changed over the centuries. Many popular designs had long, pointed toes stuffed with sheep's wool for stiffening. By about 1400, fine shoes worn outside the home were protected by **pattens** — thick overshoes, somewhat like **clogs**, that were made of wood and leather.

Garters tied around pants legs helped block drafts and keep legs warm.

This fashionable men's shoe was made in about A.D. 1400 from fine, soft leather by expert **cordwainers**, or leatherworkers.

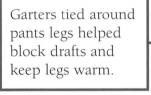

Asia

The peoples of Asia created many different kinds of footwear. Designs were shaped by local climates and by available materials. Wars, invasions, and migrations also brought changes of footwear.

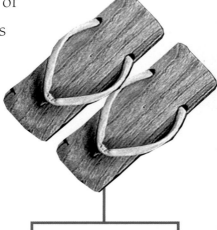

Simple Sandals

In hot, tropical regions such as Southeast Asia, many people went barefoot or wore simple, lightweight sandals. These were made of wood, leather, or braided plant fibers. Typically, they had straps running along each side of the foot from a small piece in between the toes called a toe post.

These traditional toe-post sandals have wooden soles and leather straps.

Central Asian Boots

In many parts of eastern Asia, outdoor footwear styles were based on soft, leather ankle boots worn by nomads who rode on horseback across grassy steppes. Starting in about A.D. 1200 to 1500, these styles were carried by armies of Mongol invaders from China to India and Russia. Indoors, men and women went barefoot or wore backless slippers. Slippers were also popular in western Asia.

This painting — from the Mogul dynasty that ruled northern India between 1526 and 1858 — shows typical Central-Asian-style ankle boots on the victim of an Indian elephant.

This Japanese woman and her servant girl wear wooden geta clogs with *tabi*, which are socks that have a separate space for the big toe.

Kip-Kap and Geta

For protection from rain or from garbage in the streets, women in many parts of Asia wore clogs with thick wooden soles that raised their feet at least 2 inches (5 centimeters) above dirty ground. In Japan, such clogs are called **geta**. These clogs often had names that echoed the sound clog-wearers made as they clattered along. In Turkey, they were called *kip-kap* or *kub-kob*.

Tiny shoes, often beautifully embroidered, were made to fit noble Chinese women's bound feet.

Lily Feet, Crippled Beauty

Beginning in about A.D. 900, the custom of foot binding spread among noble families in China. Young girls' feet were gradually bent and tightly bandaged to create "lily" feet. For almost 1,000 years, bound feet — a sign of women's high rank and beauty — made walking painfully difficult. Their lily feet made it impossible for women to walk far from home.

Who invented the first nonslip footwear?

15

In many parts of southern Africa, ordinary men and women did not wear shoes. Most went barefoot. Their feet became very strong, but they were in danger of injury from sharp stones, spiky plants, snakes, and stinging insects.

Tanzanian sandals help protect feet.

Sandals for Safety

Simple sandals — consisting of a flat sole fastened to the foot with straps or ties — protected feet from stepping on sharp objects. Most were made of tanned leather or rawhide. Sandals' shapes depended on local fashions, which were flat and wide in western Africa, but rounded and curved in eastern regions. They usually fastened with leather strips across the instep, around the back of the heel, and sometimes over the big toe. The finest sandals were decorated with brightly colored patterns painted on the leather.

Rain-Forest Clogs

In equatorial Africa and dry, desert regions, such as the Horn of Africa in the northeast, sheep and cattle do not thrive. Leather was not easily available for making sandals or shoes, so artisans made footwear from wood instead. African clogs featured a thick, flat sole decorated with carved patterns. A toe post, topped by a wide wooden ball or cap, helped wearers keep the clogs from flopping off their feet.

These wooden clogs from Tanzania have carved toe posts to keep the clogs in place.

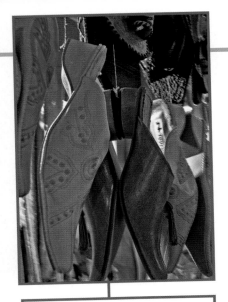

Modern backless slippers from northern Africa hang for sale in a market.

Camel Boots and Slippers

In northern Africa, good foot protection was needed when walking over hot sand or riding camels through the desert. Many northern African men and women wore flat, backless slippers influenced by Middle Eastern designs. They removed them before entering their homes or, because most were Muslims, before going into mosques to say prayers. Desert nomads wore calf-length boots for long camel journeys. These boots had thick leather soles; those woven by Tuareg women had legs of colorful woolen fabric.

What other materials were used to make African footwear?

Fit for a King

Footwear was expensive and, therefore, became a status symbol. It also featured in several traditional rituals. For example, kings of the Ashanti people (now of Ghana, in western Africa) were believed to be too important and too holy to set foot on the ground. Kings' servants carried them everywhere, and kings' feet were protected by special shoes. Other West African rulers, such as kings of the Yoruba people (now of Nigeria), also wore fancy footwear as signs of their special status.

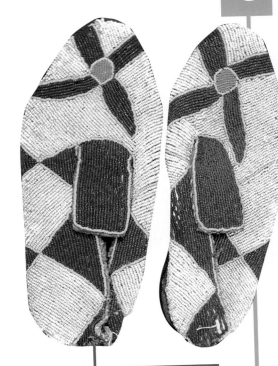

Yoruba royal boots and shoes such as these are richly decorated with beads that cover their entire surfaces.

17

Early Americas

The continents of North and South America provide some of the most extreme and varied environments on Earth. The Native American peoples who lived there developed many different kinds of footwear, made from local materials, to deal with these extremes.

Gold and Feathers

In South America, the Incan peoples of the Andes Mountains made boots of llama skin for protection against the cold. For Incan royalty, some boots were covered with thin sheets of real silver or gold. Ordinary Aztec people went barefoot or made sandals of cactus fiber. In battle, Aztec warriors and nobles wore padded leather shin guards and leather sandals decorated with feathers.

Aztec sandals usually fastened at the front of the foot with decorated laces.

Inuit and Aleut Boots

Inuit and Aleut people lived in the far north of North America, where the ground is frozen for most of the year, then boggy in the summer months. They made two different kinds of boots, plus indoor slippers of soft, furry hare skin. Winter boots were made of caribou skin or sealskin, fur side outward. Placing the fur on the outside helped produce a non-slip sole. Summer boots were made of thinner

Men's boots, made in Alaska, have sealskin soles and reindeer skin uppers and are decorated with seal intestine, dog hair, and wolverine fur.

caribou skin. Tiny stitches pulled very tightly created almost waterproof seams.

Native American hunters dance on top of snow with the help of snowshoes in different shapes.

Walking on Snow

In the cold northern regions of North America, Native peoples made special shoes to allow them to hunt for food when deep snow covered the ground in the cold winter months. Snowshoes have frames of wood or antler with sinews or thin strips of leather laced across them. They spread the wearer's weight over a much wider area than the sole of a human foot and so prevent wearers from sinking into the snow. Snowshoes are still used today.

How did Native Americans prepare animal hide to make shoes?

Moccasins

In the woodlands and grasslands of North America, shoes called *makisin*, now called **moccasins**, were made from single pieces of buckskin that were gathered together around the top of the foot. The buckskin was made with the fur side inside to create a warm lining. For extra insulation, dry grass might also be packed inside. Sometimes a flap was added to cover the upper instep, and a wide cuff was added to wrap the ankle warmly.

These nineteenth-century moccasins were made in a traditional design. They are decorated with the kinds of colored glass beads Indians obtained when trading with European settlers.

19

After about A.D. 1500, the gap grew greater between elaborate new styles — worn by rich, high-ranking people — and rough, simple shoes worn for work by ordinary men and women. Men's footwear was fancier than women's because their feet were seen. Women's shoes were hidden by long, full skirts.

Duck Bills

Medieval pointed shoes were replaced by shoes with extremely broad toes, nicknamed **duck bills**. They were often made of fragile luxury materials, such as silk or velvet. In the early sixteenth century, some shoes were **slashed**. This decoration reflected high-fashion clothes worn by rich, powerful people.

King Henry VIII of England (reigned 1509–1547) wears embroidered, silk, square-toed shoes with stockings.

Boots and Spurs

For most of the seventeenth century, Europe was at war. Fashions reflected military styles, such as tall leather boots with thick soles and turnover "bucket" tops, originally designed to protect soldiers fighting on horseback. Underneath tall boots, men wore over-the-knee stockings trimmed with lace or fringe that was designed to be seen. High-ranking men added spurs, a sign that they were officers or knights.

A young man shows one of his spurs on his bucket-top boots. This boot style was popular at the English royal court in about 1640.

High Heels

After about 1650, high heels became popular for boots, shoes, and slippers worn by men and women. Heels first became popular in France but soon spread to many parts of Europe. Heeled footwear was made of leather and often covered in silk or velvet. It might be decorated with gold or silver buckles, large ribbon rosettes or bows, or jewels and embroidery.

This embroidered and beaded silk shoe sports a sloping French heel.

How did French heels get their name?

Wooden Clogs

Ordinary people could not afford high-fashion footwear. Working men and women continued to wear plain shoes that had changed very little in design since the early Middle Ages.

They also wore wooden pattens, or slip-on clogs. Both of these styles were cheap, hard wearing, and good for keeping feet warm and dry when working on wet or frozen ground. With clogs, men and women wore thick, knitted stockings, usually made from natural, cream-colored wool. Men sometimes also wore **gaiters**, or shaped, cloth leggings.

A painting of a couple from the Pyrenees Mountains in southern France shows the man wearing traditional clogs. The woman wears plain, flat, black-leather shoes.

Western World 1750–1900

The years from 1750 to 1900 saw great technical and economic changes in Europe and the United States. New social groups, the working class and the middle class, developed. Their lifestyles were reflected in their footwear.

Boots for Heroes

In 1776, the United States declared independence from Britain. To try to keep the U.S. in its empire, Britain hired troops from the Hesse region of Germany. These soldiers wore distinctive knee-high **Hessian** boots. In the U.S., this style developed into the heeled boots worn by cowboys. In Britain, this German boot became the basis of the tough riding boots first worn by the Duke of Wellington.

This nineteenth-century cartoon makes fun of the design of the first **Wellington boots**.

A WELLINGTON BOOT

Spatterdashes

Fine shoes were expensive and very delicate. Beginning in the 1600s, men and women protected their shoes and stockings up to the knee with thick, strong leggings called **spatterdashes** or gaiters.

By the nineteenth century, gaiters fell out of fashion. They were replaced by a short, ankle-length **spat** that filled the gap between the top of a shoe and the bottom edge of a pants leg or skirt hem.

Spats were made of stiffened fabric in white, tan, or gray. They buttoned neatly on one side and were held firmly in place by a buckled strap that passed under the instep.

Our Home Sweet Home

Middle class families — who made their money from running businesses or working in the professions — placed great value on maintaining spacious, comfortable, peaceful homes. After returning home from work, men liked to relax in easy, backless slippers or house shoes. House slippers were made of soft, fine leather; **felted** (boiled until compressed) wool; **tapestry**; or velvet.

This pair of nineteenth-century gentleman's slippers is embroidered with gold stitching.

Sweet and Simple

For most of the nineteenth century, shoes worn by fashionable women were light and delicate. Outside, they wore high-heeled ankle boots made of kid (baby goat) leather that fastened at the sides with rows of tiny buttons. Indoors, they wore low-heeled slippers made of silk or fine leather. This delicate fashionable footwear was a great contrast to the sturdy wooden clogs and hobnailed, leather, front-laced boots worn by working-class women. When women wore delicate shoes, they showed people that they did not belong to the class of women who worked for a living.

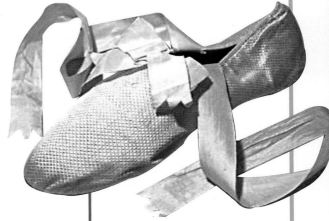

This nineteenth-century woman's silk slipper was fastened by ribbons tied around the ankle.

What were Wellington boots made of?

Western World 1900–1950

The early twentieth century was a troubled time. Millions of young men died in two world wars (1914–1918 and 1939–1945). Millions more families faced poverty, hunger, and homelessness during the economic crises of the 1920s and 1930s. Many people felt lucky to have any shoes to wear, but fashions changed fast for the fortunate few.

Functional Footwear

At work and in wartime, ordinary men and women wore machine-made, low-heeled, thick-soled, lace-up leather boots. Soldiers' boots were similar but heavier and with hobnailed soles that were put onto the boots with extra nails. Many people could only afford one pair of boots or shoes, so they looked after them carefully.

Some men and boys found low-wage work running shoe-shine stalls.

Short-Skirt Styles

Women's lives changed fast in the early twentieth century. They won the vote, trained for careers, and took over men's work in wartime. They cut their hair short and wore short skirts. For the first time in thousands of years, their legs were on display! Fashion shoes were designed to flatter legs. Popular styles had medium heels, tapering toes, and straps called bars across the instep to hold them in place.

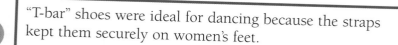

"T-bar" shoes were ideal for dancing because the straps kept them securely on women's feet.

Neat Feet

Smart footwear was an essential part of the stylish, tailored look favored by fashionable young men with money. For business and for city life, they wore polished **Oxfords** (neat, lace-up shoes). For casual wear, they wore boots or **brogues** (heavy, laced shoes decorated with fancy stitching, punched-hole patterns, and tassels). **Loafers** (slip-on shoes) and spectator, or **co-respondent**, shoes (made with different colored leathers) were also fashionable.

These two-colored co-respondent shoes for men, made in about 1930, are decorated with punched holes and zigzag edging.

1900 — 1950

Sports and Leisure

At the start of the twentieth century, men and women wore laced, leather boots for outdoor sports such as football and cycling. For sports played indoors or in the summer, such as basketball and tennis, they wore lighter shoes with canvas uppers and flexible, cushioned, rubber soles. Manufacturers created a whole new kind of footwear based on these sportswear designs. Called **sneakers**, they were comfortable, easy to wear, and fairly inexpensive. They became very popular with young people.

The Keds® brand of sneakers was launched in the United States in 1916. By the 1930s, as this shop window shows, there were many different styles.

25

Western World 1950-2000

Until the late twentieth century, high-fashion footwear was only worn by rich, privileged people. Then, mass media rapidly spread information about changing styles. Mass-production methods made fashionable footwear cheaper and more widely available than ever before.

Starting in the 1960s, young men in Britain wore *bovver* boots — larger-than-life copies of traditional working boots.

New Meanings, Old Styles

New ways of working — in offices and automated factories — meant that, for many, heavy work boots were no longer required. Most men and women wore shoes. As a sign of rebellion, exaggerated versions of traditional workers' styles became fashionable among some young people. These boots were often made in bright colors or flimsy materials and were worn as a joke or to mock authority. Hiking boots and combat boots were also popular but more practical.

High Fashion

New footwear materials, such as metal and molded plastic, made it possible for manufacturers to mass-produce women's shoes with extremely thin, high heels. These caused

High heels caused an outrage when they first appeared. The shoes were often banned from buildings because some people feared that spiky heels would damage the floors.

an outrage when they first appeared in the 1960s. High heels can cause health issues, such as shortened tendons, dislocated backs, and foot problems, but in spite of this, they remain popular.

Musician Ace Frehley of the glam-rock band Kiss wears futuristic stage makeup, a science fiction-style tunic, and silver platform boots.

Attention Please!

Popular music performers discovered that an outrageous appearance onstage often increased their appeal. Many commissioned artists, designers, and other creative people to produce individual stage costumes, including shoes.

Designer Knockoffs

Space exploration inspired top shoemakers to design both the flat, square-toed, leather, space-age boots that were made to be worn with miniskirts of the late 1960s and puffy, extra-warm "moon boots." Top shoemakers charged high prices for their custom-made creations, but almost anyone could afford mass-produced copies.

Amusing "jelly" shoes made of soft, colored plastic were first made by exclusive designers. Mass-produced versions like these (*above right*) were so cheap that they could be worn a few times and then thrown away.

27

Global Styles Today

Today, some poor people in developing countries still have no shoes to wear. Others, who work in traditional occupations like farming, still wear old-style boots and sandals. In rich, developed nations, however, there is a wider range of footwear than ever before.

High Tech

Today, people from wealthy nations take more vacations than their ancestors and spend more of their income on recreational activities, such as skiing, hiking, or diving. These sports require specialized footwear for comfort and safety. Most recreational footwear is made of synthetic materials and relies on advanced technology.

Molded-plastic ski boots support skiers with foam padding, nylon linings, and metal-alloy **bindings**.

Specialized Styles

New technology has also helped develop footwear for all kinds of occupations. Deep-sea divers wear boots weighted with lead, firefighters have heat-proof footwear, and electronics workers wear dustproof foot coverings. Professional and amateur athletes also wear special boots and shoes. These can be difficult — and dangerous — to wear outside sports grounds, but they have inspired fashion footwear, from high heels to bedroom slippers.

Soccer boots have spikes, studs, or curved blades fitted to their soles to give extra grip on wet, muddy fields.

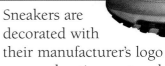

Sneakers are decorated with their manufacturer's logo — an advertisement and status symbol.

Jogging Power

Sports shoes, especially running and jogging shoes, have also inspired today's most popular footwear — mass-produced, brand-name sneakers. These are worn by adults and children for all kinds of activities at home and outdoors. They are mostly made of synthetic materials with cushioned soles and elaborate fastenings. New designs are made and promoted every year to increase sales.

International Mix

For business, most adults in developed nations still wear sober styles — laced shoes or slip-ons for men, medium-heeled **pumps** (closed-toed shoes) for women. Many children also still wear plain, simple shoes or boots for school. For vacations, parties, or relaxing with friends, people can now chose from a wide variety of styles. Today's high fashion styles often blend designs and decorations from all around the globe.

Designed in Europe in 2005, these summer sandals were made in Asia but decorated in African and Native American styles.

One of the first types of specialized footwear, ballet shoes keep dancers on their toes.

What are the most popular style of shoes around the world today?

29

Glossary

afterlife continued existence after death

artisans people who make hand-crafted goods such as pottery, jewelry, and leather goods such as belts, shoes, and boots

bark the outer layer of a tree trunk

bindings fastenings that attach ski boots to skis

brogues thick, heavy shoes, designed for country wear; often decorated with stitches, punched hole patterns and tassels

calcaei leather laced shoes worn by wealthy Romans.

caliga a type of boot worn by Roman soldiers (a pair are called a *caligae*)

clogs thick, strong, backless shoes made of entirely of wood or with wooden soles and cloth or leather uppers

cordwainers name formerly given to expert leatherworkers in Europe, especially those who worked with cordovan leather, which is made from horsehide

co-respondent two-color shoes for men, fashionable in the early twentieth century

duck bills flat shoes with very wide toes, fashionable in the early sixteenth century

felted describes a kind of wool that has been boiled until it compresses into a thick cloth

gaiters waterproof, fabric leg coverings (also known as spatterdashes)

geta wooden clogs worn by women in Japan

greaves shin protectors

Hessian describes high, leather boots with a notch at the top of the shin, often decorated with a tassel, originally worn by German troops fighting in the United States in the 1770s and 1780s

hide the skin of cattle and other large animals, such as deer or buffalo

hobnailed studded with metal nails to give extra strength and toughness

instep the top side of the foot between the toes and the ankle

lace a thin strip of hide or leather or a narrow strip of braided thread, usually tied to another lace

laced fastened with laces

leather animal skins that have been cleaned and treated (by drying, smoking or with chemicals) to preserve them

legging leg covering made of woven cloth, knitted fabric, leather, or sheepskin

loafers flat, slip-on shoes with a flat piece of leather covering the instep

moccasins shoes made of a single piece of leather, gathered around the foot, worn by Native North Americans

mules backless shoes with no covering for the heels

Oxfords dressy, flat, lace-up shoes typically with four sets of holes for laces

palm fronds the long, thin leaves of date palms and similar trees

papyrus reeds that grow in the Nile River and that can be made into a strong paper

pattens mules or overshoes with thick wooden soles designed to keep the wearer's feet warm and dry; sometimes called clogs

pumps women's medium- to high-heel shoes with plain uppers and rounded toes that grip the foot at the heel and toe

slashed cut with tiny slits to reveal an inner lining that is often a different color

sneakers sports shoes with rubber soles and cloth uppers

sole the bottom part of a sandal, boot, or shoe that touches the ground

spat a short gaiter that often fastened at the side with buttons

spatterdashes waterproof, fabric leg coverings, also known as gaiters

tanned colored and preserved by soaking in chemicals

tapestry fabric featuring a woven or embroidered picture or pattern

toe post a short, strong strap or stick on a sandal that stands between the big toe and the the next toe and helps keep the sandal on the foot

udones the Roman name for socks made from woven material

uppers the top parts of shoes that cover the feet

Wellington boots tall, straight-sided, waterproof boots first made for the Duke of Wellington, a British army commander, in the early nineteenth century

Answers

Page 5: at least ten — bark, grass, wood, hide, fur, cloth, silk, rubber, plastic, and metal

Page 7: they were buried under ash from an erupting volcano.

Page 9: slaughter-house workers, so their feet would not touch the blood that spilled on the floor from freshly killed animals

Page 11: in ancient Greece, 0*sandalia* was the Greek word for wooden, leather, or woven grass soles tied to the feet with leather straps

Page 13: a full 6 inches/15 centimeters

Page 15: according to Chinese legends, in about 350 B.C. poet Xie Lingyin fitted moveable wooden ridges to the soles of mountain boots to get a grip in the snow.

Page 17: braided grass and — in Cameroon — cast metal

Page 19: by rubbing it with animal brains and fat and sometimes by having women chew on it to soften it

Page 21: these kinds of heels were made popular by several rulers of France, including Louis XIV (reigned 1638–1715), who was of short stature.

Page 23 polished leather — but waterproof rubber copies of them were made by Henry Lee Norris, an American living in Scotland in about 1856

Page 25: seventeen

Page 27: stilettos, from an Italian word meaning thin, sharp knife

Page 29: sneakers

Glossary

Index